DATE DUE

People Who Have Helped the World

NELSON MANDELA

by Benjamin Pogrund

For a free color catalog describing Gareth Stevens' list of high-quality children's books, call 1-800-341-3569 (USA) or 1-800-461-9120 (Canada).

Picture Credits

Associated Press — 27, 51 (lower), 58, 59; Mary Evans Picture Library — 9; Gamma Liaison — 12; International Defence and Aid Fund for Southern Africa — 4 (both), 7, 11, 15, 18, 20 (both), 21: Ben Maclennan — 10: Eli Weinberg — 24 (both), 25, 28, 39, 40 (upper), 45, 46 (lower), 52: Jurgen Schadelberg — 31, 33, 36, 38: Dave Hartman — 53, 57 (both); Ali Kumalo — 48, 49; Magnum: Eve Arnold — 16: Ian Berry — 19 (both): Abbas — 34, 35: G. Mendel — 54-55; Peter Magubane — 23, 40 (lower), 50-51; Pictures by Tony Nutley from the TVS film *Mandela* — 43 (both); Spectrum Colour Library — 46 (upper); Frank Spooner — cover.

North American edition first published in 1991 by
Gareth Stevens, Inc.
1555 North RiverCenter Drive, Suite 201
Milwaukee, Wisconsin 53212, USA

First published in the United Kingdom in 1990 with an original text copyright © 1990 Exley Publications and Benjamin Pogrund. Additional end matter copyright © 1991 by Gareth Stevens, Inc. All rights reserved. No part of this book may be reproduced or used in any form or by any means without permission in writing from Gareth Stevens, Inc.

Library of Congress Cataloging-in-Publication Data
Pogrund, Benjamin.
  Nelson Mandela / by Benjamin Pogrund.
      p. cm. — (People who have helped the world)
  Includes index.
  Summary: Presents the life and career of the long-imprisoned leader of the African National Congress.
  ISBN 0-8368-0357-4
  1. Mandela, Nelson, 1918- —Juvenile literature. 2. Civil rights workers—South Africa—Biography—Juvenile literature. 3. African National Congress—Biography—Juvenile literature. 4. Anti-apartheid movements—South Africa—Biography—Juvenile literature. 5. Political prisoners—South Africa—Biography—Juvenile literature. 6. South Africa—Biography—Juvenile literature. [1. Mandela, Nelson, 1918- . 2. Civil rights workers—South Africa. 3. Blacks—Biography.] I. Title. II. Series.
  DT1949.M35P64 1991
  324.268'083'092—dc20
  [B]   [92]   90-24206

Series conceived and edited by Helen Exley
Editors: Samantha Armstrong and Margaret Montgomery
Series editor, U.S.: Amy Bauman
Editorial assistants, U.S.: Scott Enk, Diane Laska, John D. Rateliff

Printed in Hungary

1 2 3 4 5 6 7 8 9 95 94 93 92 91

NELSON MANDELA

Strength and spirit of a free South Africa

by Benjamin Pogrund

Gareth Stevens Publishing
MILWAUKEE

Above: After twenty-seven years in prison, Nelson Mandela was released on February 11, 1990. Mandela, shown here with his wife, Winnie, is thronged by supporters.

Right: Nelson and Winnie Mandela greet a cheering crowd at London's Wembley Stadium on April 11, 1990, giving the African National Congress (ANC) salute. That day, an estimated one billion television viewers from over sixty countries tuned in to witness his release from prison.

Freedom

At 4:17 P.M., Nelson Mandela walked through the gates of the prison. He raised his right hand in a clenched-fist salute. He was free.

A pent-up world had been waiting for Nelson Mandela. The moment of his release from prison on Sunday, February 11, 1990, was recorded by hundreds of journalists waiting outside South Africa's Victor Verster Prison. Television cameras instantly carried the scene to an estimated one billion viewers around the world, broadcasters gave excited descriptions to millions of radio listeners; reporters scribbled notes and cameras whirred for the next day's newspapers.

Rarely before had anyone coming out of jail received such massive attention. Never before had so many people throughout the world waited for their first sight of a person whose name was a household word, but whose face and voice were to some unfamiliar. Only that morning had the first photograph of him in more than a quarter century appeared. Now the world wanted to see him.

The cameras showed a tall man, his hair white, his face lined, but his body taut and upright. He walked smoothly and deliberately, carrying his seventy-one years lightly. Dressed in a smart, well-cut suit, he hardly looked like a man just stepping out of jail after twenty-seven years.

The first impression of strength given by his appearance was confirmed two hours later when he spoke to the world from the city hall in Cape Town, the city near the southern tip of the African continent. His voice was firm as he began: "I greet you all in the name of peace, democracy, and freedom for all."

The fact that Nelson Mandela had spent twenty-seven years in prison for his political beliefs was reason in itself for the intense interest in him. Even more, he

"During my lifetime I have dedicated my life to this struggle of the African people. I have fought against white domination, and I have fought against black domination. I have cherished the ideal of a democratic and free society in which all persons live together in harmony and with equal opportunities. It is an ideal which I hope to live for and to achieve. But if needs be, it is an ideal for which I am prepared to die."

Nelson Mandela, in his statement at the Rivonia trial, October 1963

had repeatedly been offered release, but had steadfastly rejected it because of his commitment to his cause — freedom for the black people of South Africa and the destruction of apartheid.

Apartheid

Apartheid is a policy of segregation and discrimination based on skin color. This policy has ranked as one of the great crimes of this century. The Republic of South Africa invented the word and applied it on a scale unknown anywhere else, putting the country in the international spotlight.

The word *apartheid* (pronounced "apart-hate") comes from the language known as Afrikaans and means "separateness." The word first became known to the world in 1948. That year, the National party, representing Afrikaners, was elected to govern South Africa and began to toughen up racial segregation. All whites had the right to vote, but people with darker skins generally did not, even though they formed the majority of the population.

In fact, apartheid began in South Africa long before 1948. It dates back to the seventeenth century, when the Netherlands was a powerful trading nation. At the time, its Dutch East India Company controlled a vast commercial empire around the Indian Ocean. Much travel throughout this empire was done by sailing ship. Because these voyages were long, demanding, and dangerous, the Dutch established a halfway refreshment station at the Cape of Good Hope. On April 6, 1652, three ships and ninety men under the command of Captain Jan van Riebeeck arrived at the chosen site. Their orders were to make it possible for the company's ships "to refresh themselves with vegetables, meat, water and other necessities by which means the sick on board may be restored to health." Cape Town now stands where this station was established.

Permanent settlement

The refreshment station was not meant to be a colony, but it rapidly became a permanent settlement, drawing a variety of settlers. By the early 1700s, the white population totaled more than 1,500 people. Many of these settlers were Dutch, but some were German, and

a small group were French Huguenots. These Huguenots were Protestants fleeing religious persecution in France. Another one thousand people in the settlement were slaves that had been brought in.

As farming spread, the settlers came into conflict with the native Khoikhoi. These people, known for their light yellow skin, lived as shepherds, moving around the countryside with their cattle and sheep. The initially friendly trading between the settlers and the Khoikhoi degenerated as the Europeans' farms crowded into the natives' land.

The Khoikhoi fought against the loss of their grazing land. It was an unequal struggle. The settlers had guns, while the Khoikhoi had only bows and arrows. In a short time, the Dutch began to hunt down the Khoikhoi as if they were animals, killing hundreds at a time. The same fate awaited another native yellow-skinned people known as the San.

Within only a few years of the start of European settlement, the pattern for South Africa's future was already in place as white people became the overlords and people with darker skins became their servants.

The Afrikaner Nationalist government took power after winning a whites-only election in 1948. The first cabinet, shown here, established the policy of apartheid, or racial separation. Racial prejudice already existed in South Africa, but even in places where the local white community peacefully coexisted with the black community, the Nationalist government separated them.

Very early on, another racial group emerged as the European and native people mixed. This large group of mixed-race people became known as "Coloured."

Dislike of authority

In 1795, Britain occupied the cape and brought in its own settlers. An English-speaking group of Europeans now grew alongside that of the Dutch. The Dutch settlers wanted to be left alone and had already developed a tradition of fighting against authority. Having the British at the cape was difficult for them because their rulers were now foreigners. They had still more reason for grievance when, in 1833, Britain abolished slavery throughout the British Empire.

For many of the Dutch farmers, known as Boers, this was too much. In 1835, they set off from the cape area on a journey that came to be called the Great Trek. Slowly driving their ox wagons over the mountains and across the dry veld, the Boers pushed their way north into Africa's interior. In this new land, the Boers carved out the independent states of Transvaal and the Orange Free State. Another state, Natal, fell under British control in 1843.

The Boers led lonely, hard lives. Suspicious of the outside world, they put their trust instead in the culture that was developing within their states. They practiced their own religion — the stern Calvinist religion developed in Europe. They developed and spoke their own language, called Afrikaans, which developed primarily from Dutch but was influenced by German, French, English, and several African languages. They even began calling themselves Afrikaners. They no longer kept slaves, but their black servants were kept in a lowly state at the mercy of the employer. And as they moved inland, the Boers had discovered a new cheap work force in the brown-skinned Bantu people.

The greatest warriors

Through the first half of the nineteenth century, southern Africa was in turmoil as black tribes fought each other for land and supremacy. The first black people whom the settlers met — as early as 1702 — were the Xhosa in the eastern part of the region. In the interior were other nations, including the Sotho, the Pedi, and the

Even the fierce Zulu warriors could not stand up to the guns of the British army. The Zulu were defeated in the Battle of Ulundi in 1879. But it was not only a military loss; British soldiers burned and destroyed many villages as well, as this drawing from the time shows.

Swazi. But the greatest warriors were the Zulu, in what is now the province of Natal on the east coast. Shaka, a Zulu king of the early nineteenth century, led his people through many fierce battles, many of which were victories for the Zulu. Shaka was a cruel leader who killed those who opposed him. As part of his military training, Shaka made his soldiers learn to run barefoot by making them run over fields of thorns.

The settlers and the British became part of these battles, fighting tribes and setting one tribe against another. Gradually, the superior weapons of the white fighters put them on top. By the time of the last great battle — in 1879 when British troops broke the might of the Zulu army — many native people had been driven into ever-smaller areas of land and most of their cattle had been seized or were dead. To survive, the people had to get jobs on the white settlers' farms or seek help from the missionaries.

Up to this point, South Africa had consisted of a series of small agricultural communities. But this

changed when two discoveries pushed the region into the industrial era. The first discovery was made in 1866 when a farmer found a giant diamond — one of the biggest ever discovered. Prospectors rushed in from all over the world to make their fortunes.

To reap the diamonds from the earth, the white miners needed many laborers. The pattern already established on white-owned farms carried over here as well: white bosses enlisted black people to do the manual work for little pay. White miners made sure things stayed this way by allowing only white people to get licenses to dig for, and to deal in, diamonds.

"City of Gold"

Twenty years later, in 1886, a second discovery was made: gold. Again, fortune hunters poured into South Africa. In the midst of the gold rush, the city of Johannesburg mushroomed into existence. To Zulu, it became eGoli — "City of Gold."

Miners dug shafts and tunnels to get at the seams of gold that ran deep into the ground. This required many more workers, and the natives were again enlisted. White miners, many of whom came from Europe, made sure that they kept the skilled work and most of the wealth for themselves. Even though blacks earned little, the poverty in the rural areas was so bad that the mines drew them like a magnet.

As mining grew, so did the need for still more hands. White miners introduced certain measures to force black men to leave their homes in the remote countryside and come to work in the mines. One method used was a poll tax. Every black man was required to pay this tax each year or go to prison. To raise the necessary money, many of the local men were forced to get work outside the black tribal areas.

Systems of control

Gradually, rules were applied to keep the wives and children of the workingmen in their country homes. The men were allowed to go and work for only as long as they were needed, after which they had to return home. A bureaucracy of officials, police officers, prosecutors, magistrates, and prison wardens gradually came into existence to direct black lives.

Above: With the discovery of diamonds in South Africa, thousands of people flocked to the mines. White workers did the skilled jobs, while black workers did the pick-and-shovel work for much less money.

Opposite: Johannesburg has not been a city of gold for everyone. Many black workers coming from the rural areas have had to live in harsh conditions, as seen in this compound. Apartheid laws did not allow these migrant workers to bring their wives and children to the city. Millions of black families were separated in this way.

11

Mahatma Gandhi's tactic of nonviolent resistance to unjust laws was developed and practiced during the years he spent in South Africa. When it formed in 1912, the African National Congress adopted Gandhi's methods. But in South Africa, police tactics (captured here in a scene from the movie Gandhi*) were so repressive that the technique failed.*

Residential segregation was already the rule. White families lived in their own suburbs in the new towns, while a distance away, black people lived in their overcrowded, poverty-stricken, disease-ridden areas that were without proper water or sewage facilities.

The diamond fields, which had originally been occupied sparsely by native people, were under Britain's colonial wing. However, the gold bonanza was in the heart of the South African Republic, one of the several republics created by Boers after conquering the native black people. The Boers were horrified by the influx of the white immigrants that the diamonds and gold had lured. Not only were these newcomers foreigners, but they demanded a say in government in return for paying taxes.

The Boer War

Tension mounted, and Britain intervened. In 1899, the Boer War broke out. Within a few months, British

troops captured the Transvaal cities of Johannesburg and Pretoria, the capital. It seemed the war was over. But many Boers refused to give in. They stubbornly turned to commando tactics, fighting on horseback behind British lines.

To combat them, Britain drafted another 250,000 soldiers and resorted to harsh tactics, including a scorched-earth policy. By this policy, British troops destroyed Boer farms and burned their crops. The soldiers also put Boer women, children, and elderly men into concentration camps that claimed over 26,000 lives before peace was signed in 1902.

The war left scars that shaped the future. The Boers were embittered by their defeat and their suffering. They hated Britain and foreign influences even more than before. Their feelings intensified because, at first, British officials tried to suppress the Boers, sulking at their language. Children who spoke the Boer language — Afrikaans — in school classes were made to stand in a corner wearing a dunce cap. But Boer-Afrikaners were determined to survive as a people.

Eventually, Britain turned to encouraging reconciliation between the two main white groups — the Afrikaners and the English-speaking people. On May 31, 1910, the Union of South Africa came into being as a dominion of the British Commonwealth. As a dominion, South Africa was considered a self-governing nation under the British monarch.

Within this union, black people were by far the majority, but Britain agreed with the white leaders that blacks should have only second-class status. Blacks, they declared, could not vote, and, because of this restriction, they became aliens in their own country.

Other races also suffered. The mixed-race people, or "Coloureds," were shunted aside. Asians, another group that was now part of the population, were not allowed to vote either and needed permission to travel between different parts of the country. Many Asians had been brought from India by the British in the nineteenth century to work in Natal's sugarcane fields.

Birth of the African National Congress

Blacks resented their inferior status. This resentment led blacks to form the South African Native National

Congress in 1912. It was later renamed the African National Congress (ANC). The ANC pleaded with the government to give black people a fair share in the country. It even begged Britain for protection against the white government, but Britain spurned the request. Instead, the South African parliament enacted laws that further infringed on the rights of the black majority.

In one of the first and most devastating measures, the government strengthened segregation in mining by introducing the idea of "job reservation." This idea specified that black miners could not do skilled work. Skilled jobs were reserved entirely for white miners. This principle of different jobs for different groups was an injustice that would cause decades of suffering.

A broader law, the Native Land Act of 1913, deprived blacks of their farms and homes and restricted them to special areas known as "native reserves." By this act, the South African government allocated more than 90 percent of the total land to the white population of one and a quarter million, while less than 7 percent of the land was set aside for the four million blacks. South Africa's black people found themselves dispossessed in the land of their birth. Later, the law was extended to stop blacks from buying land in the towns.

More segregation laws

But some blacks were necessary to the cities. Further laws ordered cities to provide segregated residential areas for these blacks. These run-down, isolated areas were called townships. Blacks lived in the townships as long as their services were required. Town councils, all of which were run by whites, expelled "surplus" blacks — that is, black people whose work was no longer necessary to the whites.

In time, methods of controlling the movement of black families were refined. At the heart of the controls were the pass laws. Blacks were required to carry an identification document, or pass, at all times. This pass noted into what areas a black person had permission to travel. Policemen could stop a black person at any time and demand to see this pass. If caught without a valid pass, he or she was instantly arrested, prosecuted, and sent to prison. Over ten million people would be prosecuted under the pass laws during the coming

decades. Black men also had to carry receipts to show that their tax payments were up to date.

Control was strengthened by laws giving the government almost limitless power in black areas. The government could order any black person — or even an entire nation — to leave home and move somewhere else. It could also order a person or a national group to remain within a specified place. Thus, building on a 250-year-old pattern of white-black relations, the rule over black people grew tighter and more restrictive.

Nelson Mandela is born

Into this situation, Nelson Rolihlahla Mandela was born on July 18, 1918. In accordance with custom, he was given a European name, Nelson, as well as a name in his native Xhosa language. His Xhosa name, Rolihlahla, means "stirring up trouble."

His father, Henry Gadla Mandela, was a chief of the Xhosa-speaking Tembu tribe. Chief Mandela was

The African National Congress formed in 1912 to secure rights for black people. Two years later, it sent representatives to Britain to beg for protection against white rule in South Africa. For almost five decades, the African tribal nations of South Africa, under the leadership of the ANC, would use nonviolent resistance in their fight for a fair deal. Not until 1961 was violence first used.

wealthy enough to own a horse and to have enough cattle for four wives. He had twelve children. Nelson and his three sisters were the children of his third wife, Nosekeni, or Fanny.

Nelson Mandela was born in the Transkei reserve of South Africa. His village, Qunu, was a collection of beehive-shaped huts with thatched roofs, known as rondavels. It was a quiet, tranquil existence. Qunu was a long way from anywhere, especially in those days when local roads, if they existed, were unsurfaced.

Nelson, his mother, and his sisters had three huts. One hut was used for sleeping, and everyone slept on mats on the ground. Another hut was used for cooking, and the third hut was used for storing food. As a married woman, Nosekeni had her own field to tend and her own cattle kraal — an enclosure for cattle made from thorn bushes. Almost as soon as Nelson began walking, he helped look after the family's cattle and goats. Relatives remember that he loved animals and,

Rolling hills blanket the Transkei — the region where Nelson Mandela was born. The land is beautiful, but in many places, it supports too many people. Cattle and erosion have caused severe damage.

while herding, he would speak to each cow by its name, as if speaking to a friend.

His mother could not read or write, but she wanted Nelson to be educated. So he soon started as a pupil at the local school, which had classes for only the younger grades. Nelson was noted as a quiet, industrious boy who did not live up to his Xhosa name.

When Nelson was ten, his father died. Henry Mandela's relative, Chief Jongintaba, then looked after Nelson as if the boy were his own son. In the same way, Jongintaba accepted responsibility for Nelson's education. In Xhosa society, this was a natural thing. Jongintaba was the head of the family clan. By custom, all members of the clan were treated like people in the same family because they were all descended from the same ancestor. Nelson, or anyone else, could go to the home of any relative, whether in the same village or in a village miles away, and know that he would get food and shelter as his due right.

"Almost every African household in South Africa knows about the [1921] massacre of our people at Bulhoek in the Queenstown district when detachments of the army and police, armed with artillery, machine guns and rifles, opened fire on unarmed Africans, killing 163 persons, wounding 129, during which 95 people were arrested simply because they refused to move from a piece of land on which they lived."
Nelson Mandela, speaking at a conference in Ethiopia, February 1962

The Great Place
So in 1928, Nelson moved to the Great Place, which was the royal kraal at Mqekezweni. There he shared a rondavel with his cousin, Justice.

The school at Mqekezweni was a small, rough building that was short on everything from space to supplies. For example, two classes were held in one room at the same time, and children wrote on slates because they had no notebooks. Here Nelson's studies included English, Xhosa, geography, and history.

Each day after school, Nelson and Justice went to the fields to look after the cattle. In the evening, the boys drove the cattle back to the kraal for milking. When this was done, Nelson often sat near the fire and listened to the community's elders speak about "the good old days, before the coming of the white man." The elders spoke of that as a time when their people could move freely over the country and when they had their own king and government. They told Nelson tales of the wars their ancestors had fought to defend their territory and of the warriors' acts of courage.

These years formed Nelson's character and shaped his attitudes. Learning the history of his people fostered Mandela's commitment to helping them.

A feast

When Nelson graduated from primary school, the clan celebrated it in the traditional manner: a sheep was slaughtered for a feast.

But primary school was not to be the end of Nelson's education. Jongintaba sent the boy first to Clarkebury, then to Healdtown — top high schools for black pupils — and then to college at Fort Hare.

South Africa's educational system, like so many facets of life there, discriminated against nonwhite people. Authorities made sure that there were separate schools for whites and blacks, as well as for Coloureds and Asians. The government spent at least ten times more on white children than on black children. The results were obvious in the schools. Enough money was spent on white schools so that education could be made compulsory. But it wasn't the same for blacks. Many black children never went to school at all. Many of those who did dropped out at an early age. Black children such as Nelson Mandela, who actually got as far as high school, belonged to an elite group.

Life at Healdtown followed a specific schedule. As a boarder, Nelson lived in a dormitory that was little more than rows of beds and small lockers for the boys. The beds themselves were straw-filled mattress covers. At 6:00 A.M. each morning, the students rose to the sound of a wake-up bell. After a quick wash in cold water, the boys had breakfast, which consisted of a mug of hot water with sugar and a piece of bread. Lunch was the big meal, and the students ate lots of beans with maize porridge. Sometimes lunch included a small piece of meat. Supper was the same as breakfast. On Saturdays, the students were allowed to walk to the nearest village. There, students who could afford it bought fish and chips.

Religion played a strong role in Mandela's life at Healdtown. Even before this, he had always gone to church regularly. At Healdtown, he took part in the evening prayers as well. On Sundays, he went to church and to Scripture lessons.

In 1938, twenty-year-old Nelson Mandela finished his schooling. He had done so well that Chief Jongintaba decided he should go to the university — the South African Native College at Fort Hare — not far from

Healdtown. The college was also racially segregated. Most of its three hundred students were blacks, but Coloureds and Asians also attended.

Like any student, Mandela soon discovered that there was much more to attending the university than study. Tall and good-looking (especially in the three-piece suit that Chief Jongintaba had had tailored for him), Mandela was popular with the other students. His interest in dancing made him especially well liked among the women.

Suspended from the university

Living conditions at Fort Hare were more comfortable than those at Healdtown. The food, however, was often of poor quality. Although the students frequently complained about it, nothing was done. This led Mandela into his first protest action: he was involved in a strike. The college authorities suspended him.

Jongintaba told Mandela to apologize to the university authorities so that he could return to his studies. Young Mandela refused to do so. Instead, he and Justice ran away to the city of Johannesburg, hundreds of miles to the north. To raise money to get there, the two young men sold two of Jongintaba's oxen to a local trader. Jongintaba was extremely angry. He tracked the runaways to Johannesburg and the gold mine where Mandela was working as a mine policeman. Jongintaba ordered them to return home. Justice had to go back, but Mandela asked Jongintaba to let him remain in Johannesburg so that he could study law. Jongintaba agreed.

Johannesburg

Mandela was accustomed to rural life and the smallness of Fort Hare. Suddenly, he was immersed in the bustling, vital city of Johannesburg. Although not more than fifty years old, Johannesburg ranked as South Africa's largest city. Mandela found it both exciting and bewildering. In the northern part of the city, white families lived in large houses, with pleasant gardens filled with trees and flowers. Not all whites lived this way, but even the more modest houses were far better than the houses of black families. For black people, existence was at its most vibrant in townships

When Mandela arrived in
Johannesburg, he lived
in a township. There was
no electricity and no
running water, and he was
surrounded by poverty,
crowded housing, and
much suffering. It was at
this time that he joined the
ANC and dedicated his life
to helping his people in
their struggle for equality.
Both Mandela and the
ANC knew that equality
would come only when
there was a true form of
power sharing — one
person, one vote.

like Sophiatown and Alexandra, where blacks could still own land, even though these townships were crowded, squalid, and rife with crime.

It was 1941 when Nelson Mandela, aged twenty-three, arrived in Johannesburg. World War II had started two years earlier, and South Africa had sided with Britain against Nazi Germany. The war stimulated industry. The country suddenly needed factories to produce everything from armored cars to boots and cigarettes for soldiers. In turn, factories needed vast numbers of workers. Workers streamed in from the reserves, swelling the already crowded townships.

For the black South Africans, this was a time of excitement. With war underway against Nazism, talk of democracy was in the air. The government was trying to get black men to join the army — although they were not allowed to carry arms — and held out the possibility of a new deal in the postwar era. Black people looked hopefully to the future.

About this time, the ANC experienced a renewed popularity. Over the preceding thirty years, the group's existence constantly swung between popularity and decline. It had been in a low state when the group elected a new president in 1940. The new president was Dr. Alfred B. Xuma, a medical doctor who had studied in Britain, the United States, and Hungary. He changed the ANC into a modern political movement and put life into it once more.

Marriage for Mandela

Nelson Mandela enjoyed the excitement and energy of Johannesburg. He lived in Alexandra — a township on Johannesburg's outskirts — struggling to survive on very little money. Resuming his studies, he graduated with a bachelor of arts degree by correspondence and trained with a white lawyer, Lazer Sidelsky. Sidelsky took a keen interest in the progress of young Mandela and became like an older brother to him.

It was also in Johannesburg that Nelson Mandela met Walter Sisulu. Sisulu and Mandela got along well together, starting what would be a lifelong friendship. Although they did not know it then, Mandela and Sisulu would one day become key black leaders in South Africa.

During the early 1960s, a host of African countries achieved independence from colonial rule and wearing national dress became popular. In this picture, which was taken during one of his trials, Nelson Mandela wears national dress.

"Groomed from childhood for respectability, status, and sheltered living, he was now thrown into the melting-pot of urban survival."
    Mary Benson, in her book
    Nelson Mandela: The Man
    and the Movement, *on
    Mandela's arrival
    in Johannesburg*

Sisulu had an enormous influence on Mandela's life — both professionally and personally. On a personal level, Sisulu invited Mandela to stay with his family in Orlando, another of Johannesburg's townships. There, Sisulu introduced Mandela to a cousin, Evelyn Mase, a nurse from Transkei. Romance blossomed between Evelyn and Nelson, and they married in 1944.

The young couple had very little money, so there was no traditional wedding feast. Nor could they find anywhere to live until, once more, African family generosity came into play. Evelyn's sister, brother-in-law, and two children lived in three tiny rooms. They offered one of these rooms to the newlyweds. No one expected any pay for the hospitality.

Family life

After a while, the government allocated Nelson and Evelyn Mandela a house of their own in Orlando. It was now the Mandelas' turn to support other family members. Mandela's sister came from Qunu to Orlando to attend high school. She was the first of a stream of visitors, including Mandela's mother, who came from the Transkei. Visitors were welcome to stay for as long as they needed to, and the house was often crammed with people. Somehow, though, it always seemed big enough for everyone — even when, the following year, Evelyn gave birth to the Mandelas' first child, a son whom they named Thembi. Nelson and Evelyn would have yet another son, Makgatho, and a daughter, Makaziwe, in their marriage. Sadly, another daughter died when she was just nine months old.

Mandela enjoyed his family. He enjoyed coming home at night, bathing the babies, and sometimes cooking. He was also keen on physical fitness. Early every morning, before anyone was stirring in the streets, he jogged for a few miles. He began going to a gymnasium and took up boxing as well.

But there was much else to do outside of his home life. While Evelyn worked as a nurse to support the family, Nelson continued his law studies at the University of the Witwatersrand, or "Wits." Most students there were white. The university allowed only a few black students to attend, and they had to be exceptional. Even so, they had second-class status: they attended classes and lectures, but could not take part in sports or social activities. But Wits, like Cape Town University, at least admitted black students. Most other "white" universities did not.

At Wits, Mandela studied for a second degree — a bachelor of law so that he could work as a lawyer. He struggled to cope. When one of his professors criticized an essay he had written, an upset Mandela confided to a fellow student: "I'd like to see how he would manage writing essays by oil lamp at night in a [township]."

In fact, life in the townships was much tougher than that. Like most other black families, the Mandela family was packed into a tiny house. The whole house was probably about the size of a large living room in a European or U.S. home. It did not have hot water or a modern toilet.

Travel proved another problem with living in the townships. Mandela spent much time traveling to and from the university because of the inadequate bus service. Even when he was inside the city, he could not ride on just any bus. He had to wait for the special buses marked for "non-whites."

With only two bread winners in the Dabula family, the evening meal is shared fairly. There are twenty-five family members crammed into a four-room house. In many township houses, eight children share a bed.

African Nationalists

Walter Sisulu's second major influence on Nelson Mandela was to introduce him to the African National Congress. Mandela was soon actively working with a group of young men who were striving to take the organization into radical action. At a meeting in Johannesburg in 1943, these men formed the ANC Youth League. This group became the means of pushing for change inside the parent body. Its members did much to inspire African nationalism, which promoted Africa's black culture as equal in importance to that of the whites. These African nationalists believed that black people had to prepare for outright confrontation with the white rulers. Only this, they said, would break the pattern of white domination.

They also argued for "non-collaboration" — for black people to refuse to take part in segregated bodies created by the government. They said, for example, that black residents should refuse to sit on advisory boards for the townships. The boards, the Youth League felt, had no power and were meant to be black rubber stamps for the decisions made by white officials.

Racial signboards such as these mushroomed because of apartheid. Left: In the 1950s, a Johannesburg tram stop is marked for "Native," or black, passengers. Segregation existed on Johannesburg's buses and trams even before apartheid was introduced. Right: After 1948 and the start of apartheid, signs like this became common at railroad stations throughout the country. Only in 1990 did such signs become illegal.

African nationalists also opposed black cooperation with people of other groups. They singled out for special suspicion the white and Asian people who were members of the Communist party. They rejected communism as an alien ideology.

Mandela in opposition

At the same time, Nelson Mandela was moving in other, contradictory circles. Despite restrictions on the social life of the university's black students, he often met with white and Asian friends whom the Youth League opposed. He was finding that he liked these people and made deep, lasting friendships with some of them.

Mandela also enjoyed the intense political debates he often had with these people. He plunged into the avid debates about how best to achieve freedom for the black majority. His mind, trained and sharpened by his legal studies, made him a natural leader — especially when allied with the warmth that, by now, was characteristic of him.

By 1947, Mandela was a recognized figure in the Youth League, and he was elected to the key position of general secretary. But then came 1948. This was a year that would forever change South Africa. Nothing was to be the same after it. In May, Dr. Daniel François Malan became prime minister and the Afrikaner National party came into office as the government. These Afrikaner Nationalists were elected by the overwhelmingly white electorate on the promise of apartheid. The party planned to extend this policy of racial segregation that was already so much a part of South Africa. The aim was nakedly summed up in the Afrikaans word *baaskap* — which means "to be the boss." Whites were the bosses.

Racial pigeonholes

The new government immediately set about putting its policies into practice. At the heart of it was the Population Registration Act, which put every single person into an official racial pigeonhole, ranging from white through Coloured, Asian, and Chinese. Every black person was "classified," as it was officially called, according to his or her tribe.

Some white people put up their own signs. The insulting warning of this notice was made worse by the use of the word kaffir, *which was, and is, an abusive term for black people.*

For years to come, this classification opened the way to all sorts of abuse, with vicious individuals reporting Coloureds to the authorities. Families were split by it: one person might be classified white, while a brother or sister might be declared Coloured. When this happened, members of the same family were not able to live together.

Racial laws poured out. They began by outlawing marriage between people of different groups. Then the Group Areas Act divided every inch of the country into segregated residential and business areas. Only people of a specified race could live or own a business in a specified area. As experience was to show, time and again, the white people grabbed the best land for themselves and ordered blacks, Coloureds, and Asians to live somewhere else. Over 3.5 million people were deprived of their homes, farms, and shops in this way. Armed policemen dealt with anyone who resisted being moved.

In the 1950s, this division of land became even more defined with the introduction of a plan to turn the already established native reserves into Bantustans, or "homelands." According to this plan, all black people not employed in urban areas were to return to the "homelands" to which they had been assigned. Eventually the "homelands" were to become self-governing. In practice, the arid "homelands" served as reserves to hold the blacks whose services were not required in the cities.

Enforcing apartheid

The apartheid system took hold of the country. The pass laws were made tougher, and the number of arrests of blacks soared. Signboards went up everywhere in both Afrikaans and English, stating: "Net blankes — whites only." Racial separation now applied to every train and bus in the country. Black workers were prohibited from going on strike. Some jobs, such as house painting and carpentry, were ordered to be for white workers only. "Job reservation" was now reinforced by law.

Most public facilities were also controlled by the system. In the universities, it restricted black students. Parks in cities were closed to all nonwhites, and so

White people did not have to carry a pass, but, by law, black men always had to have one. The pass was a small book — similar to a passport — that contained a photograph of the bearer, details of his birth, and information about where he was allowed to live and work. Thousands of black people were arrested for not having a pass or for being in a city without permission. In the 1950s, the government forced black women, as well as men, to carry the pass.

were libraries. The beaches on the seashore were segregated. Usually the best and the safest beaches were reserved for whites. Concert halls and theaters were closed to people who were not white, even in those few parts of the country where strict apartheid had not previously applied.

In schooling, the government decreed not only separate schools, but also an inferior education for blacks. Dr. Hendrik F. Verwoerd, who later became prime minister, said bluntly that if a black pupil "in any kind of school in existence is being taught to expect that he will live his adult life under a policy of equal rights, he is making a big mistake. There is no place for him in [South Africa's] European community above the level of certain forms of labor."

To deal with opposition, the government enacted the Suppression of Communism Act. This act, which banned the Communist party, also gave the government the power to ban other organizations — and people.

"Who will deny that thirty years of my life have been spent knocking in vain, patiently, moderately, and modestly at a closed and barred door? What have been the fruits of moderation? The past thirty years have seen the greatest number of laws restricting our rights and progress, until today we have reached a stage where we have almost no rights at all."

Chief Albert Luthuli, president of the African National Congress, 1952

Over the years, many hundreds of people would be "banned," which meant that their personal liberty was severely restricted, even though many of them were actually anticommunist. Harsh as this law was, it was but the first in a chain of statutes aimed at curbing opposition. The laws eventually allowed the government to arrest whomever it pleased and to keep people in jail without trial for as long as it pleased.

Suppression gathers pace

As suppression was gathering pace, Nelson Mandela played a key role as the ANC Youth League's general secretary in putting the organization on a national footing. The group's immediate aim was to make the Youth League an effective pressure group inside the ANC. This was achieved. By the end of 1949, it succeeded in having the ANC national conference adopt the "Programme of Action" — an outline of action to oppose white rule based on noncollaboration.

At this time, Nelson Mandela's views seemed in a state of flux. He had shared the uneasiness of many

Even while involved in politics, Nelson Mandela was a busy lawyer. For years, he and Oliver Tambo, a close friend and colleague in the African National Congress, were law partners. Their offices were filled with desperate people who needed help in protecting themselves from unfair apartheid laws.

Youth League leaders about a joint stand against racism by the ANC and the Asian community. He still had an African nationalist suspicion of influences by Asians and whites. And yet he was changing as he met people of different racial groups and outlooks.

The events of May 1, 1950, were a turning point for him. On that day, the Communist party called a strike to protest against the government's intention to ban it. Some ANC leaders backed the call, arguing that a threat to the Communists was a threat to all. Others, and especially Youth Leaguers, opposed having anything to do with the Communists.

On the morning of the strike, Mandela is said to have rushed around, urging black people to go to work. The strike proved to be only moderately successful, but it ended in tragedy. When violence stemming from the protest broke out, the police opened fire and killed eighteen people.

The deaths inflamed feelings, and a new call was issued for a day of protest on June 26. This time, the ANC gave its support. Mandela was wholeheartedly with the protest and was appointed volunteer in chief — the chief organizer of the protest. From then on, he grew even more accepting of ANC cooperation with other groups.

Mandela, the leader

Mandela was now rising rapidly to the upper ranks of ANC leadership. In 1951, he was elected president of the Youth League. In 1952, at thirty-three, he became president of the powerful Transvaal branch of the ANC, which had Johannesburg as its headquarters. At a national level, he was one of the four deputy presidents.

His professional life was also progressing. He and Oliver Tambo, a fellow member of the ANC Youth League, went into partnership as lawyers. The firm of Mandela and Tambo had offices in a small building across the street from the Johannesburg magistrates' courts. There was only a handful of black lawyers, and life was not easy for them. Even the magistrates did not give equal respect in the public glare of open court. Even so, the waiting room of the Mandela and Tambo law office was always full of people quietly waiting their turn.

"The authorities grew alarmed; in July [1950] they countered in their own macabre manner. Nelson was jerked out of bed in a pre-dawn police raid. His house was surrounded by the police. The net was cast wide. The homes of twenty other Transvaal activists were raided. They were all arrested. This was the first instance of a Nationalist technique which would become commonplace in the years to come."

Fatima Meer, in her book Higher than Hope: A Biography of Nelson Mandela

"Nelson's day was taken up by the court, so he spent the evenings, and late nights, attending to his legal practice and ANC work. As a result he usually returned home when the clock had started counting in the new day; in addition, he rarely spent weekends with the family."

Fatima Meer, in Higher than Hope: A Biography of Nelson Mandela

Even getting the offices was an achievement because, under apartheid, most black people were not allowed to occupy offices in the city. They had to go to black areas — even if, for lawyers, that meant being miles away from the main courts. In fact, the government ordered Mandela and Tambo to quit their downtown offices since their presence there violated the Group Areas Act. They appealed and somehow obtained permission to remain.

Challenging the government

But Nelson Mandela did not have much time to run a legal practice. He was again appointed volunteer in chief for the ANC's next major challenge to the government, the most ambitious protest in its history. Planned in 1951, the protests were set to begin the following spring unless South Africa's government scrapped six "unjust laws," including the pass laws and the Suppression of Communism Act. When the government refused, the ANC launched a Defiance Campaign urging all South Africans to violate racial laws. The ANC's plan was to pack the prisons with violators of these unjust laws.

More than eight thousand people responded during the next few months. Some sat on park benches marked "whites only." Black and Asian protesters entered post offices through "whites-only" doors, and a white volunteer broke the law by going into a township without permission.

Even Mandela was arrested, but he paid bail so that he could continue to organize the campaign. He went up and down South Africa, speaking at hundreds of meetings, small and large. He urged people to defy the laws, constantly reminding them that this was to be a nonviolent protest.

Nonviolence was one of the ANC's principles. ANC leaders believed in peaceful protest as a result of their Christian outlook. They were, in addition, influenced through their contact with the South African Indian Congress (SAIC) and the lessons of resistance taught by Mahatma Gandhi. Gandhi had fought against racial discrimination while in South Africa early in the century. He had pioneered nonviolent direct action as a method of protest that he later used to free India.

Nonviolence was also practical politics. The South African police carried guns and were quick to shoot. Mandela was striving to avoid giving them reason to open fire. But despite the ANC's best efforts, violence did erupt, from both the police and township people.

The campaign was called off when the government enacted a law making defiance of apartheid a far more serious crime. Thus, for example, someone who sat on the "wrong" park bench could be fined, whipped, or imprisoned for up to five years. People who persuaded others to break the law received even stiffer penalties.

Mass police raids

In what was to become a familiar pattern in the years to come, the police carried out mass raids on homes and offices of ANC and SAIC officials. They seized many

The police have been the enemy of black South Africans for as long as Nelson Mundela can remember. As the enforcers of apartheid laws, the police have often treated black people cruelly. This picture shows policemen beating demonstrators. Although it was taken in the 1970s, such violence was common throughout the course of the ANC's nonviolent struggle.

documents and arrested twenty-two of the protest's leaders, including Mandela. The leaders were accused of promoting communism, which, under the Suppression of Communism Act, was illegal.

At their trial, the accused were found guilty and sentenced to nine months in jail. But the judge said he realized that they had consistently tried to avoid violence. Because of that, he suspended the sentences on the condition that they did not repeat their crimes.

Although he was free, Mandela was now truly in the firing line. Along with other leaders, he was a target for government harassment. Among other restrictions, the government ordered the leaders not to attend any meetings. Mandela, treated even more harshly, was also ordered not to leave Johannesburg for six months.

This attempt to silence Mandela's political voice was only partially successful. Although he could not attend the ANC's regional conference in Transvaal in 1953, he wrote a speech that was read for him at the gathering. His speech revealed a great deal about the difficulties being faced in opposing the government.

"The masses had to be prepared and made ready for new forms of political struggle," he said. "We had to recuperate our strength and muster our forces for another and more powerful offensive against the enemy. To have gone ahead blindly as if nothing had happened would have been suicidal and stupid.

"The old methods of bringing about mass action through public mass meetings, press statements, and leaflets calling upon people to go to action have become extremely dangerous and difficult to use effectively."

Through the 1950s, the ANC relied more on words than on mass organization as it continued to be the victim of government harassment. During this time, many South Africans still hoped that the government could be persuaded to modify apartheid laws. They believed that this was possible through peaceful means. So despite the difficulties and dangers involved in protests, the ANC did not abandon them.

The effects of three hundred years of prejudice, intensified now by apartheid, could be seen among both white and black people. Jules Browde, a white friend of Nelson Mandela, remembers telling Mandela of an incident from his own life. Browde and his wife were going out one night, and their four-year-old son, who was being looked after by their black maid, cried: "I don't want to be left with a black face."

"We don't know why he speaks like that," Browde told Mandela. "We are liberal people, and there is no trace of racism in our home."

Mandela told him he had been in the same situation —in reverse—with one of his children. White friends had come to visit at the Mandela home. When they left, one of Mandela's children asked him: "Why do you have white people here?"

Mandela said that he had replied: "Not all white people have white hearts. Some have black hearts."

Fighting back

It was a troubled time for the ANC. No one could stand up to the all-powerful government as it forged ahead with apartheid. In the early 1950s, the government extended its power by taking control of black education. The educational system the government then established was known as Bantu Education.

Black education to this point had been in the hands of the churches and missions. The government was opposed to this system because it encouraged the idea of equality between blacks and whites. The problem with this kind of education, declared Hendrik Verwoerd, then minister of native affairs and the creator of the Bantu Education system, was that it created "wrong expectations on the part of the Native." The government's system, Mandela and many other blacks pointed out, was an education for inferiority.

The new Bantu Education was another hurdle for Mandela and the ANC. In response to it, the ANC called for boycotting the schools. But it was ill-prepared for such a step. Many parents wanted alternate schooling for their children before they would go along with the boycott. The few who listened to the ANC and boycotted paid a heavy price: the government punished them by denying their children readmission to school.

Banned

In September 1953, thirty-five-year-old Mandela's active political role came to an end — or so it seemed. A new set of banning orders not only confined him to

In 1952, using new dictatorial powers, the government ordered Nelson Mandela not to leave Johannesburg and not to attend any meetings. When he did not obey the orders, he was prosecuted. He is seen here in court after being given a suspended sentence of nine months' imprisonment.

In the South African gold mines, black miners and white miners have always been treated in very different ways. Black miners, who form more than 90 percent of the total work force, usually lived in crowded men-only compounds, such as that shown above. In contrast, white workers lived with families and enjoyed pleasant housing with low rents. Opposite: An aerial picture of a village for white miners.

Johannesburg, but they also instructed him to resign from the ANC and a host of other organizations. He was also forbidden to attend gatherings: he could not attend political meetings or even social gatherings such as dinner parties or dances.

Although this curbed his public presence, Mandela refused to recognize the validity of the bannings. That was the ANC's attitude, too. The government was banning many leaders and the ANC responded with the slogan: "We stand by our leaders." In practice this meant that whenever a leader was banned, he or she outwardly resigned from the organization but secretly remained a member. This was a risk for Mandela and the others. They could be jailed if caught.

Working now behind the scenes, taking care to hide what he was doing from the police and their network of informers, Mandela was involved in planning for a Congress of the People. This meeting, held in Johannesburg on June 26, 1955, brought together

thousands of people. Mandela, in disguise, watched the meeting from a house nearby.

On the second day, he saw the police storm in, seize every document they could find and, working into the night, question everyone present. Despite this, the meeting unanimously approved the now-famous Freedom Charter, a document which set out demands for a democratic South Africa for all living there.

The Freedom Charter

The Freedom Charter was drawn up from ideas suggested by people from all over South Africa. Its purpose was to give clear definition to the goals of the freedom movement. The following points make up the democratic changes that the charter demanded:

> The people shall govern!
> All national groups shall have equal rights!
> The people shall share in the country's wealth!

TREASON TRIAL

The ACCUSED

DECEMBER 1956

The land shall be shared among those who work it!
All shall be equal before the law!
All shall enjoy equal human rights!
There shall be work and security!
The doors of learning and of culture shall be opened!
There shall be houses, security and comfort!
There shall be peace and friendship!

The charter concluded with the following statement: "Let all who love their people and their country now say, as we say here: 'These freedoms we will fight for, side by side, throughout our lives, until we have won our liberty.'"

The Freedom Charter was a moderate document that set out elementary rights and hopes. But to the government, it was a dangerous and subversive document. The government took nearly eighteen months to strike back. Then, before dawn on December 5, 1956, Mandela awoke to heavy knocking at his front door. It was a squad of armed policemen. They searched his home and arrested him.

Mandela, Walter Sisulu, and Oliver Tambo were among the 156 people of all colors arrested in this raid. All were charged with high treason. If found guilty, they could be hanged. By the end of the month, the prisoners were released on bail, but their trial dragged on and on. The team of prosecutors tried to prove that the accused had been working to overthrow the government for a communist state. Almost the entire leadership of the ANC and its allies were pinned down by the trial. They spent every weekday in court and hours after each session consulting their lawyers.

The trial would last four and a half years.

Winnie Mandela

These years saw the transformation of South Africa, and of Mandela's life. In fact, the year 1956 introduced a major change in his life when his marriage to Evelyn ended. The pressure of his political life had taken its toll. After moving to Natal to study midwifery, Evelyn asked for a formal separation. She and Nelson were divorced in 1957.

Mandela's personal life had been suffering for some time. There wasn't much time left between the

Opposite: In mass police raids during December 1956, 156 people of all groups were arrested and charged with plotting to overthrow the government of South Africa. The marathon trial that resulted, known as the Treason Trial, dragged on for over four years. Nelson Mandela, by this time a leader in the African National Congress, was one of the accused. In this group photograph, he can be seen in the middle of the third row from the bottom.

"The [Freedom] Charter is more than a mere list of demands for democratic reforms. It is a revolutionary document precisely because the changes it envisages cannot be won without breaking up the economic and political set-up of present South Africa. To win the demands calls for the organization, launching and development of mass struggle on the widest scale."

Nelson Mandela

Nelson Mandela married Winnie Nomzamo Madikizela, a social worker in Johannesburg, on June 14, 1958.

treason trial, secret ANC meetings, and his legal practice. His only personal time was often used jogging in the mornings or going to the gym.

After his separation, Mandela was introduced to a young social worker, Winifred ("Winnie") Nomzamo Madikizela, and she became part of his hectic schedule. When they decided to marry in 1958, they had to get police permission because Winnie wanted the ceremony, in traditional fashion, to be held at her home in the Transkei. Mandela was given permission to leave Johannesburg for four days.

"I knew when I married him that I married the struggle, the liberation of my people," Winnie has said.

That early understanding was to help sustain her in the hard years that followed. She had to get used to the way that he was accessible to people. Wherever he was — walking in the street or eating in a restaurant — people would come up to him, either merely to say hello or to seek his help.

He always listened. Each person was made to feel that he or she had Mandela's total attention. Each person was treated with respect.

The ANC splits

Meanwhile, the ANC was having problems of its own. The more immediate problems concerned the growing crisis inside the ANC. While Mandela had come to accept interracial cooperation, some of his African nationalist colleagues grew more alarmed as the ANC's ties deepened with other racially exclusive bodies. They were all working for a multiracial South Africa, but each of the races had its own organization.

The African nationalists argued that the ANC did not oppose apartheid strongly enough and that it had deserted the Programme of Action and non-collaboration. The nationalists also condemned the Freedom Charter as a meaningless stunt.

Their grievances gathered strength in the absence of the ANC's chosen leaders. Because of the many bannings and trials, the ANC's leadership was often in a state of chaos. Its finances were also often in a mess. In 1959, the disputes led to a break led by Robert Mangaliso Sobukwe, who had worked with Mandela in the Youth League. A new group, known as the Pan-Africanist Congress (PAC), was formed.

One of the PAC's first actions was to attack the pass laws. During the 1950s, South Africa's pass laws were ferociously enforced, with hundreds of arrests each day, and more than 300,000 convictions each year. To black people, the pass was their badge of slavery. Only black people had to have passes, and only black people were arrested on the spot if they could not show passes to a policeman. The laws were enforced so harshly that people were often arrested while standing outside their own homes — despite protesting that their pass was a few feet away.

The Sharpeville Massacre

Sobukwe's new PAC accused the ANC of not taking concrete action against the unjust laws. Announcing that he was launching "decisive action," Sobukwe called on blacks to leave their passes at home and to offer themselves for arrest. He led the way on Monday, March 21, 1960. In only a few places did large numbers respond to his call. But in the PAC stronghold of Sharpeville, near Johannesburg, Sobukwe's call was answered by fifteen thousand people. The huge

Nelson Mandela burned his pass after Chief Albert Luthuli, president general of the ANC, called on black people throughout South Africa to burn their passes to protest government repression.

crowd gathered at the Sharpeville police station, where police officers opened fire on the unarmed people. In the course of the tragedy, 69 people were killed. Another 180 were wounded.

The massacre put South Africa on the front pages of newspapers everywhere. Inside the country, it set off mass anger. Mandela was among the ANC leaders who publicly burned their passes. The ANC called for a protest strike a week later and drew the biggest response ever known. As violence erupted, the police shot more people. In Cape Town's townships, the police went from door to door, beating people into returning to work.

The government tottered and declared a state of emergency that enabled it to do whatever it wanted. Immediately, it arrested thousands of people, mainly blacks. This included Mandela and other key political leaders, who, while still at the Treason Trial, were seized and kept in jail without trial for nearly five months. Then, in April, it outlawed the ANC and PAC. After that, merely to be found with an ANC or PAC lapel badge could lead to twelve months in jail. Rather than disband, however, the banned organizations went underground. By this time, however, many black leaders were disillusioned. They had supported the idea of nonviolence for so many years, "knocking in vain, patiently, moderately, and modestly at a closed and barred door," as the ANC's last legal president, Chief Albert Luthuli, put it. Yet they were ignored, banned, jailed, driven out of the country, or, as had happened at Sharpeville, shot down.

As a final attempt to follow a nonviolent route of protest, fourteen hundred delegates gathered for what is now known as the All-In-Africa Conference in March 1961. Out of the conference, held in the town of Pietermaritzburg in Natal, came a demand that a national convention of all South Africans be held to prepare a new, just constitution. A National Action Council was formed to present the demand to the government. Along with it went the declaration that if the government failed to meet the demand, a three-day work strike would take place at the end of May.

A surprise key speaker at the conference was none other than Nelson Mandela. No one had realized that Mandela's banning orders had expired. He had been out of the limelight for so long that many in the crowd did not appreciate who he was. He was not a fiery orator and did not arouse the audience, but the mere fact that he had been present, and that he was the leader, stirred up a hornet's nest. The police swarmed around but could not find him. He had left as soon as he had given his speech.

The Black Pimpernel

After the conference, Mandela returned to the Treason Trial in Pretoria. On March 29, 1961, after over four years of legal battle, he and the thirty others accused were found not guilty and freed. From there, as he had announced at the conference, Mandela took his work underground. Unless he worked in secret, Mandela believed, he would be unable to continue his work.

After this announcement, Mandela left his home and went into hiding. Moving around the country, he began organizing the upcoming three-day strike when the government rejected the plea for a new constitution. If he was nervous about being caught, he did not show

"When a government seeks to suppress a peaceful demonstration of an unarmed people by mobilizing the entire resources of the state, military and otherwise, it concedes powerful mass support for such a demonstration. We plan to make government impossible. . . . I am informed that a warrant for my arrest has been issued and that the police are looking for me. . . . [I] will not give myself up to a government I do not recognize."
Nelson Mandela

"I have had to separate myself from my dear wife and children, from my mother and sisters, to live as an outlaw in my own land. I have had to close my business, to abandon my profession, and live in poverty and misery, as many of my people are doing. I shall fight the government side by side with you, inch by inch, and mile by mile, until victory is won. I will not leave South Africa, nor will I surrender. The struggle is my life. I will continue fighting for freedom until the end of my days."
Nelson Mandela, describing life "underground"

"The time comes in the life of any nation when there remains only two choices — submit or fight. That time has now come to South Africa. We shall not submit, and we have no choice but to hit back by all means in our power in defense of our people, our future, and our freedom."

From a statement issued by Umkhonto we Sizwe, December 16, 1961

it. He was calm and determined to organize the strike. In the following months, he escaped capture many times and was nicknamed the "Black Pimpernel," the man the police could not catch.

All the while, he kept in touch with the public through a few journalists whom he trusted. Sometimes, he phoned them from telephone booths to read them press statements. At other times, he met them at night, often wearing a simple disguise, such as that of a night watchman. Nelson Mandela, the well-dressed lawyer, became a workingman who melted into the background.

The government put the police on guard against the three-day strike. Leaders were arrested. Meetings were prohibited. Black workers were threatened with loss of their jobs if they stayed away from work. These massive pressures ensured that the strike was only partially successful.

The extent to which the government went to destroy the strike and to crush the call for a national convention proved the last straw for Nelson Mandela. This was the great turning point. As he later revealed, in June 1961, he and some colleagues "came to the conclusion that, as violence in this country was inevitable, it would be unrealistic and wrong for African leaders to continue preaching peace and nonviolence at a time when the government met our peaceful demands with force."

What he was referring to was a secret meeting attended by representatives of the African National Congress and the Communist party at which they agreed that nonviolent protests had proved useless. They also then agreed that it would be necessary to switch to violent resistance. This meeting marked the birth of an underground sabotage movement, Umkhonto we Sizwe, or "Spear of the Nation."

Sabotage

Umkhonto we Sizwe struck its first blow with a series of bombings on December 16, 1961, the day observed by Afrikaners each year to mark victory over the Zulu in the Battle of Blood River in 1838. The sabotage was aimed at damaging property such as power lines, power plants, and government buildings. Killing people was totally avoided. Only years later would bombs be set off with the aim of killing people.

A few weeks later, Mandela slipped out of the country. He did not have a passport and went through Botswana to travel to other African countries, meeting leaders and seeking help in attacking apartheid. He wanted financial aid and training for guerrillas. Sympathetic African countries like Ghana listened and promised support. Mandela returned to South Africa six months later, recrossing the border at Botswana. The South African police heard he was back, and the hunt for him was on again.

His underground base was a farm called Lilliesleaf in Rivonia, a suburb of Johannesburg. Hoping to find Nelson, the police had been watching Winnie and raided her home several times. But even under their noses, she and their two daughters, Zindzi and Zeni, had managed to visit him.

Mandela moved around the country building the new organization, often in disguise as a chauffeur, "David Motsamai." But as he was driving out of the city of Durban one Sunday morning, August 5, 1962, a police car forced him to pull over. Two other police cars were behind. They knew who he was; they had been tipped off that he was coming on that road.

The police were excited about their big catch. Mandela was taken to Johannesburg and charged with inciting black workers to strike and with leaving the country illegally. He was sentenced to five years in jail. As the sentence was passed, Mandela defiantly turned to the packed public gallery, raised his fist, and shouted "Amandla!" ("Strength!")

Conditions at the Pretoria Central prison were rough. Because of apartheid, blacks had it worst of all. Mandela was given a shirt, sandals, and khaki three-quarter pants known as tsotsi shorts. The clothing was named for the *tsotsis*, the name given to teenage gangsters in townships. At that time, black prisoners were not given socks or shoes and always had to wear their tsotsi shorts despite the intense winter cold in the prisons.

After he had been in prison just a few months, Mandela and three other political prisoners were driven to Cape Town in a truck. The trip took a night and most of a day. All the while, the prisoners were handcuffed and shackled to each other. A bucket inside the truck served as their toilet. In Cape Town, they were transferred to a boat for an hour's sail to Robben Island, a maximum-security prison.

Trouble at Rivonia

But Mandela hadn't been at Robben Island long when there was a dramatic political development. On July 11, 1963, a dry cleaner's van drove up the long driveway of Lilliesleaf in Rivonia. Policemen and dogs raced out of the vans. They arrested sixteen people whom they found there, including Walter Sisulu, who had gone underground several months before. The police were triumphant. They had tracked down the high command of Umkhonto we Sizwe.

On the basis of documents found at Lilliesleaf, Mandela was brought back to face new charges with nine others in the Palace of Justice at Pretoria. He was

Winnie Mandela leaves court during Mandela's trial. Mandela was already serving a five-year prison term, but during his sentence he was tried on still more charges and resentenced. He would not come home to Winnie and his children for another twenty-seven years.

listed as accused number one. The group was charged with organizing sabotage and trying to organize a violent revolution.

In a lengthy statement during the trial, Mandela set forth his thinking. Explaining why he and others had started Umkhonto we Sizwe, he said: "Firstly, we believed that as a result of government policy, violence by the African people had become inevitable, and that unless responsible leadership was given to canalize and control the feelings of our people, there would be outbreaks of terrorism which would produce an intensity of bitterness and hostility between the various races of this country which is not produced even by war.

"Secondly, we felt that without violence there would be no way open to the African people to succeed in their struggle against the principle of white supremacy. All lawful modes of expressing opposition to this principle had been closed by legislation, and we were placed in a position in which we had either to accept a permanent state of inferiority, or to defy the government. We chose to defy the law."

Life imprisonment

The Rivonia defendants, as they came to be known, were found guilty in June 1964. Because of the serious charges, the group could have faced death sentences. Instead, they were sentenced to life imprisonment.

This time, Mandela and others in the group who were black or Asian were flown to Cape Town by military plane to be ferried back to Robben Island. That's where Nelson Mandela would spend the next eighteen years of his life. The government had announced that the sentences of political prisoners would not be reduced. Murders, robbers, and rapists were usually released after serving half or two-thirds of their sentences, but political prisoners were not.

Through the 1960s and most of the 1970s, prison conditions were harsh, and they, too, were affected by racial differences. The food was poor. Even the limited rations that Mandela and the other black prisoners were supposed to have — such as their teaspoonful of sugar a day — were not always provided, perhaps because of stealing by guards. Prisoners slept on mats on the concrete floors of their cells. A bucket in each cell

Opposite, above: Nelson Mandela was imprisoned on Robben Island, here seen from Table Mountain in Cape Town. The island's rocky coast and the cold, strong sea currents that surrounded it made it a perfect location for the maximum-security prison, which was built in the 1960s. Opposite, below: Conditions were often harsh for Mandela and the hundreds of other political prisoners on Robben Island. One of the punishing jobs they were made to do was to sit on the ground and repair old canvas mailbags.

"More powerful than my fear of the dreadful conditions to which I might be subjected is my hatred for the dreadful conditions to which my people are subjected outside prison throughout this country."

Nelson Mandela

47

Nelson Mandela's mother, Nosekeni (Fanny), talks to her grandchildren about her imprisoned son.

served as a toilet. The day began at 5:30 A.M., and the tough discipline subjected the prisoners to long hours of silent work. At the end of each working day, the men had to strip naked to be searched. After supper, it was a long night in the cell.

Communication of all types was restricted. There was no radio, and no newspapers were allowed. To be caught with even a piece of smuggled newspaper drew punishment. Letters and visits were equally restricted; prisoners were allowed one of each every six months.

The prison guards were another problem with which the prisoners had to deal. Many were dishonest, vicious, and intent on breaking the political prisoners' spirit. To deal with the guards as well as the other unsatisfactory conditions of prison life, Mandela began to use some of the tactics from the freedom movement inside the prison. Through protest and persistent complaint, the prisoners brought gradual improvements to Robben Island. Eventually, the prisoners won better food, warmer clothing, and real beds. Before long, the prisoners were allowed to read newspapers and magazines and to listen to radio broadcasts.

The political prisoners established their own network of committees to deal with matters varying from internal discipline to the right to sports and education. Mandela took advantage of whatever gains he could, working to keep both his body and his mind fit. Although through the prisoners' efforts, certain exercise outlets were now available, Mandela stuck to his own fitness routines, doing push-ups in his cell each morning. He played chess and dominoes and studied to finish the law degree that he had begun at the university in the 1940s.

In prison, Mandela gained a reputation for his willingness to help everyone. It did not matter whether a prisoner was an ANC member or was from a rival movement, such as the PAC. Mandela was friendly and was available to give advice. He was renowned for his calmness and for his willingness to listen to what others had to say.

Winnie's struggle

Mandela's pain at being away from his wife and children was made worse because of the consequences of Winnie's struggles for his freedom and her own activity on the political scene. Her involvement led to her arrest on May 12, 1969. Charged under the Terrorism Act, she was held for seventeen months. This charge could have also led to the death penalty, but she was acquitted.

But even afterward, she was constantly harassed in one way or another. The police raided her home at all times of the day and night, and she was terrorized by men who attacked her. Eventually, she was banned. Restricted to Johannesburg, she was placed under a curfew on nights and on weekends. She also had to obtain permission each time she wanted to visit Nelson in prison. Since Robben Island was 950 miles (1,530 km) away, any visit was a very expensive trip.

Then she was banished to a township outside the village of Brandfort, 200 miles (320 km) south of Johannesburg. Winnie's new home, which she could not leave without permission, had no electricity, no running water, and no telephone. A public telephone booth in the village became her "office." Twice a day she went there to phone and to receive calls from friends. As with her husband, however, nothing she said could be published.

Black anger explodes

Winnie's situation was due, in part, to an explosion of black opposition that occurred a year earlier. At that time, an order that black schools make wider use of the Afrikaans language sparked widespread protests, which came to be known as the Children's Revolt. On June 16, 1976, twenty thousand schoolchildren gathered to march through the townships in protest against this plan. Again the police began shooting, killing several children. The brutality of these deaths set off a year of revolts. At the end of the year, hundreds of people, most of them schoolchildren, had been killed.

After that, South Africa was never free of protest. The protests, with their thrust for change, helped bring Mandela's name to the fore again. For many years he had been largely forgotten. But slowly, word began to get out to South Africa and to the world of the quality and strength of the man on Robben Island.

The government was among the first to recognize the danger to itself in keeping Mandela imprisoned.

"He stood head and shoulders above the others. Everyone looked up to him and respected him. When he spoke, we listened. He was patient, tolerant, and I never saw him lose his temper."
Strini Moodley, a prisoner on Robben Island

Winnie Mandela shared her husband's political beliefs and made many of the same sacrifices that he made. This picture of her was taken in 1965.

Because of the forced resettlements and migrant worker policies, South Africa's black family structure has been broken. Only 3 percent of black schoolchildren live with both parents. South Africa's problem is based on a majority of unemployed, unskilled young people.

Throughout the 1970s and 1980s, the government had quietly approached Mandela four or five times, offering him freedom. He was told that he could have his freedom if he promised to leave the country. Each time, Mandela had refused. He insisted that he would leave prison only if no conditions were attached. When released, he intended to be a free man once again doing whatever he wanted to do.

The few people who were allowed to visit him during his time in prison spoke about his courage, his

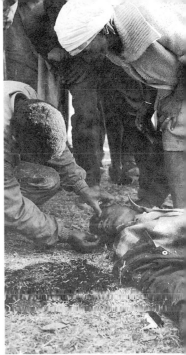

The Children's Revolt against apartheid erupted on June 16, 1976. It began in Soweto among schoolchildren but spread rapidly through the country.
Above: This was one of the victims of police bullets in the township of Alexandra, near Johannesburg.
Left: Billowing clouds of smoke mark shops and government buildings that were set ablaze as violence surged.

51

In the 1960s, the South African government clamped down on political organizations. But each time it declared one movement illegal, new ones sprang up. In the 1980s the United Democratic Front was formed as an alliance of grassroots protest groups and expressed the goals of the African National Congress. Thousands of people attended its rallies. At one rally, a youth sports a Mandela T-shirt.

wisdom, and the contribution that he should be making to resolve the deepening racial crisis in South Africa. Recognition of Mandela began to spread again. Universities, city councils, and labor unions in many parts of the world began to mark their respect for him, conferring honorary degrees on him, naming streets and squares after him, and naming scholarships after him. Governments, political parties, and international organizations started calling for his release.

To Pollsmoor Prison

Nelson Mandela's conditions changed radically. In 1982, after eighteen years on Robben Island, he was suddenly told he was leaving that prison in half an hour. With Sisulu and three other Rivonia defendants, Mandela was taken to Pollsmoor Prison — a prison set in beautiful farm surroundings near Cape Town. No explanation for the move was given. Perhaps the government feared that Mandela and his colleagues had become too powerful on the island.

His growing status was further acknowledged by the government. At one point, he had to go into a hospital for an operation. When discharged, he returned to Pollsmoor — but into a cell of his own. Then, the minister of justice began to visit Mandela. The two men liked each other, and their lengthy discussions were friendly. The guards were respectful to Mandela, even as they unlocked gates inside the jail as he passed.

But despite all of this, Mandela was still deprived of his liberty. Pollsmoor was a maximum-security prison. Mandela's cell faced inward; all he could see were the grim interior walls and a patch of sky above.

Release — but with conditions

In January 1985, South Africa's president, Pieter Willem ("P. W.") Botha, publicly offered to free Mandela. On the surface, the conditions seemed reasonable: Mandela had to renounce violence. But apartheid was still in place, and the ANC was still waging its armed struggle against white rule. Mandela felt that if he condemned violence, he would be condemning the ANC and its struggle for freedom.

In response to Botha's offer, Mandela wrote a statement and sent it to his daughter, Zindzi. In the

statement, which Zindzi read on her father's behalf at a public meeting in Soweto, Mandela declared that he would negotiate with the government only when he was a free man and the ANC was free.

"I am not less life-loving than you are. But I cannot sell my birthright, nor am I prepared to sell the birthright of the people to be free," Mandela proclaimed. The relatively short statement ended with the words: "I cannot and will not give any undertaking at a time when I and you, the people, are not free. Your freedom and mine cannot be separated. I will return."

Demands continued to be heard from around the world for his release. He was the person who represented freedom for South Africa's people. He became the symbol, too, for freedom in all parts of the world where people were oppressed.

Split inside the government

The South African government was divided over what to do about Nelson Mandela. His fight was becoming a source of terrible embarrassment to the ruling white class. He was keeping international attention focused

By 1986, the call to release Nelson Mandela and other political leaders from jail was a major issue, with crowds gathering even in small towns like Middelburg, Cape Province. Armed only with banners, people often defied police orders to disperse.

"Nelson Mandela is the power that he is because he is a great man — about that there can be no doubt. Our tragedy is that he has not been around to help douse the flames that are destroying our beautiful country."
Desmond Tutu, Anglican bishop of Johannesburg

53

on apartheid and on the unceasing violence as the white government scrambled to keep itself in power. Some members of the government did not want to release him out of fear of what a freed Mandela might do. Others argued that they had no choice.

The world's newspapers, radio, and television gave him avid attention. Every new report of his imminent release was hotly pursued. In 1988, his seventieth birthday was observed as no birthday has ever been celebrated. The highlight of the celebration was a rock concert held on July 11 at London's Wembley Stadium. The concert, which featured seventy entertainers, was attended by 72,000 supporters and watched live by millions around the world.

Suddenly, a few weeks after his birthday, it was announced that he was ill. An alarmed world waited for word as he was taken to a hospital and diagnosed as having tuberculosis. But Mandela recovered. When he was released from the hospital, the government placed him in a comfortable house at the Victor Verster Prison in the countryside 35 miles (56 km) from Cape Town. Officials offered to bring his family to him

On July 11, 1988, a rock concert at London's Wembley Stadium celebrated Nelson Mandela's forthcoming seventieth birthday. The crowds who attended the concert, as well as the millions of people throughout the world who watched the event on television, were only part of the multitudes that demanded his release.

there, but he rejected the idea. He did not want his family living in jail. Despite the comfort, he was on his own for most of the time, and his loneliness was acute.

By 1989, political events were picking up speed. The country's economic situation was grave. The economy was reeling under the impact of the nearly nonstop internal turbulence and protests, combined with the effects of sanctions applied by other countries. South Africa's newly elected president, Frederik Willem ("F. W.") de Klerk, realized that the country's economic troubles were inevitably tied to the unrest among the nonwhite population that made up the bulk of the working class. He also realized that to change this situation, he would have to deal with the leaders of the ANC and other freedom organizations. To deal with these leaders, he would have to release them.

In October 1989, President de Klerk released eight high-ranking political prisoners, including Walter Sisulu. On February 2, 1990, he announced the unbanning of the African National Congress, the Pan-Africanist Congress, and all the other bodies that had been declared illegal over the years.

Opposite, above: Nelson Mandela, unbowed by his twenty-seven years in jail, speaks at an enthusiastic "welcome home" rally in Soweto on February 13, 1990.

Opposite, below: The cheering had begun two days before when he went straight from jail to greet his supporters on Cape Town's Grand Parade.

"One person had come to embody the aspirations of all the South African people — Nelson Mandela. His life symbolizes our people's burning desire for freedom; his imprisonment is the imprisonment of the whole South African nation; the fight for his unconditional release, and that of all political prisoners and detainees, in the glorious fight against injustice, racial bigotry, and man's inhumanity to man."

Oliver Tambo, president of the ANC

Release — at last

As 1990 began, Mandela's release was only a question of time. Leaders of the black political movements went in droves to Victor Verster Prison to consult with Mandela. Finally, on February 10, de Klerk announced that Nelson Mandela was to be released the next day — without any conditions.

For this reason, hundreds of journalists waited outside Victor Verster Prison on that hot summer afternoon. For this reason, a huge throng of people gathered opposite Cape Town's City Hall for a first sight of the man whom so many in South Africa revered as the leader who would take them to freedom. And for this reason, tens of millions of people throughout the world were filled with excitement.

In his speech to the world that day, Mandela began by speaking of peace, democracy, and freedom. He ended by declaring that his commitment was unchanged: "In conclusion, I wish to quote my own words during my trial in 1964. They are as true today as they were then: 'I have fought against white domination, and I have fought against black domination. I have cherished the ideal of a democratic and free society in which all persons live together in harmony and with equal opportunities. It is an ideal which I hope to live for and to achieve. But if needs be, it is an ideal for which I am prepared to die.'"

That declaration made it clear that his release from prison was a new beginning. Without delay, he threw himself into giving content and direction to the hopes that his release had aroused. He continued to meet with leaders of the government, and the first formal talks between the ANC and the government were held. The two sides set up a joint working group to deal with the issues of the release of remaining political prisoners and the return of exiles.

Triumph and controversy

People were startled by Mandela's lack of bitterness about the past and about what he had endured at the hands of the ruling whites. As he moved from meeting to meeting, he showed sympathy for the anxieties of white people about their future as a minority group subject to majority rule.

56

In an early speech, he reaffirmed the ANC's long-standing policy calling for nationalization of industries — by which the country's government would own and control them — and the redistribution of wealth. When Mandela saw how nervous this made the white business leaders, he backed away from such statements. He evidently realized the need to make the business community feel secure, despite its track record of exploitation and support for apartheid.

Five months later, he was intent on persuading foreign business leaders how needed and welcome they would be in a future South Africa. By that time, he had softened his position, noting that the ANC "holds no ideological position which dictates that it must adopt a policy of nationalization."

Mandela made a series of triumphant visits overseas to Europe, Asia, and North America. A dozen countries within six weeks would have been a tiring schedule for even a much younger man. As fit as Mandela was, he wasn't always able to carry out the punishing schedule of meetings arranged for him. He left many disappointed people behind as appointments were canceled to enable him to rest.

His loyalty, though, led him into controversy — first when he embraced Yasir Arafat, the leader of the Palestine Liberation Organization, and then later when he praised Libya's Muammar al-Qaddafi and Cuba's Fidel Castro for their human rights records. Mandela's actions were based on the fact that these leaders had been supporters of the ANC in the years when the movement had few friends. His public backing for them was received badly in the West. The adulation with which he was received — from meetings with the leaders of countries he visited to a ticker-tape parade in New York — spared him criticism that might otherwise have been directed at him.

His trips were, however, successful in raising money to fund the ANC as it struggled to create a legal presence and to work out the details of its policies after thirty years of underground existence. The overseas trips also enabled Mandela to persuade some Western governments to maintain sanctions. He argued that sanctions were necessary to make sure that the white government continued to work toward ending apartheid.

The struggle at home

It was at home that his real efforts had to be made. Upon his release most people — white and black — probably had unrealistic beliefs about what he could, and would, immediately achieve. Many greatly admired his gentle and powerful manner and thought he would bring a swift end to sanctions and ensure the country's return to international respectability. They thought that he could quickly end the violence between the police and black demonstrators at one level and among black political groups at another. Nelson Mandela was not able to give them what they wanted, and many turned sour. Meanwhile, whites on the extreme right wing continued to fear him as they had always done, and threatened growing violence as their answer.

Among black people, Mandela's popularity remains as strong as ever. But even he has been unable to quell the violent struggle for supremacy between the ANC and the Zulu nationalist movement, Inkatha. Nor has he been successful in ending the killing between the ANC and other black political movements. His problem lies in the gap between Mandela the myth and Mandela the man. The first is a superhuman being who can do anything — and who does not exist. The second is a man of flesh and blood who has wisdom, talent, and commitment on a scale seldom matched in the history of the freedom struggle — and who is also a mortal being with everyday weaknesses.

It is Nelson Mandela the man who is doing his human best to end apartheid and to resolve one of the world's most acute problems.

Opposite: Nelson Mandela made a series of triumphant visits to the world's capitals. In New York, hundreds of thousands of people turned out to applaud him. He was given a traditional ticker-tape welcome — with paper thrown from skyscraper windows — as his car drove slowly through the streets.

Left: F. W. de Klerk, South Africa's president, is the man who released Nelson Mandela from jail. Personal ties, based on mutual respect, grew between the two men. Together, they have set about the task of trying to build a South Africa without apartheid.

59

For More Information . . .

Organizations

The following organizations can provide you with more information about South Africa and apartheid. When you write, be sure to tell them exactly what you would like to know. Always include your full name, age, and return address.

African National Congress of South
    Africa (ANC)
P.O. Box 15575
Washington, DC 20003-9997
(Attn: Lindwe Mabuza, Chief
    Representative, ANC Mission to U.S.)

American Committee on Africa
198 Broadway, Suite 402
New York, NY 10038

The Embassy of South Africa
3051 Massachusetts Avenue NW
Washington, DC 20008

International Defence and Aid Fund
    for Southern Africa
#200, 294 Albert Street
Ottawa, Ontario K1P 6E6
Canada

Books

Biko. Donald Woods (Random House)
Every Kid's Guide to Understanding Human Rights. Joy Berry (Childrens Press)
Nelson & Winnie Mandela. John Vail (Chelsea House)
Nelson Mandela: South Africa's Silent Voice of Protest. J. Hargrove (Childrens Press)
South Africa. Mike Evans (Franklin Watts)
South Africa in Pictures. Department of Geography, Lerner Publications (Lerner)
Sun City: The Struggle for Freedom in South Africa. Dave Marsh (Penguin)
We Live in South Africa. Preben Kristensen and Fiona Cameron (Franklin Watts)
Why Are They Weeping?: South Africa under Apartheid. Alan Cowell (text) and David
    C. Turnley (photos) (Stewart, Tabori & Chang)
Winnie Mandela: The Soul of South Africa. Milton Meltzer (Penguin)

Glossary

African National Congress (ANC)
    A multiracial organization founded in 1912 to work for equal rights for all the people of South Africa.

Afrikaans
    A language based on Dutch, with loan-words from French, English, German, and various African languages. It is, with English, one of South Africa's two official languages, spoken mainly by Coloureds and Afrikaners. Attempts to impose Afrikaans on all South Africans led to the Soweto riots in 1976.

Afrikaners
    The descendants of South Africa's Dutch settlers; also known as Boers. About 2.2 million Afrikaners make up about 60 percent of the country's white population.

apartheid

Literally "apart-hood." This is the official government policy of racial separation and discrimination in South Africa. Although South Africa's government now seems to be moving toward the eventual end of apartheid, many of its effects still remain.

Asians

In South Africa, this term is used to describe people of Indian descent.

banning order

In South Africa, a government order by which a person has his or her rights and privileges restricted. Usually a "banned" person cannot attend public meetings, belong to any group disapproved of by the government, give interviews, publish books or articles, or travel outside the country. Banning often involves a kind of house arrest as well; banned persons cannot leave their homes at night or on weekends without permission, and they cannot have more than one visitor at a time.

Bantu

A group of African languages spoken by some seventy million people, including almost all black South Africans. Zulu, Xhosa, and Tembu are all Bantu dialects. This word was formerly applied to people, but this usage is now considered insulting by most black South Africans.

Biko, Steven (1946-77)

The founder of the Black Consciousness movement and organizer of the student uprising that led to the Soweto riots. Beaten to death in prison by South African police, Biko is widely viewed as a martyr to the cause of black nationalism.

Botha, Pieter Willem (P. W.) (1916-)

Former prime minister of South Africa, under whose administration the first moves to dismantle apartheid were made.

boycott

An organized avoidance, during which people will refuse to use whatever they are protesting. A boycott often demonstrates that a business depends upon the very people it discriminates against.

Coloured

In South Africa, this term is applied to people of mixed descent. Throughout this book, the word *Coloured* has been used to mean any Afrikaans-speaking South African of mixed European and African ancestry, *white* to mean any South African of European descent, and *black* to mean any South African of African descent.

de Klerk, Frederik Willem (F. W.) (1936-)

The South African president who, in 1989, vowed to dismantle apartheid, create a more just society, and bring South Africa back into the world community. As part of this program, he unbanned the ANC and the PAC and released political prisoners, including Nelson Mandela, from jail.

Freedom Charter

A proclamation of human rights drawn up by the 1955 Congress of the People, declaring that all South Africans deserved equal rights and opportunities.

Gandhi, Mahatma (1869-1948)

An Indian nationalist leader who was a leader in the movement which gained India independence from Great Britain in 1947. As a young man, Gandhi practiced law in South Africa. His twenty-year fight there for Asian civil rights inspired the later formation of the ANC and the PAC.

"homelands" (Bantustans)

Areas set aside for black tribes, one for each major ethnic group in South Africa. Most of the "homelands" are made up of unconnected pieces of land, sometimes separated by many miles. In addition, most are arid, remote, and bare of natural resources, made up of land the white settlers didn't want.

Inkatha

The only black nationalist movement to escape banning. Headed by Chief Gatscha Buthelezi, its membership is largely Zulu. In the 1980s, a rivalry developed between supporters of Inkatha and the ANC, leading to many clashes and deaths.

Khoikhoi

The original inhabitants of most of South Africa. These nomads, caught between invading black Africans in the east and European settlers in the west, were virtually exterminated as a people. The survivors intermarried with their conquerors, and thus, many Coloureds are of part Khoikhoi descent.

kraal

A cattle corral used in tribal villages in South Africa. The word is also sometimes applied to the villages themselves.

Pan-Africanist Congress (PAC)

The black South African activist group founded by Robert Sobukwe in 1959. This group broke away from the ANC to fight for majority control of South Africa, believing that the older group had become too passive. The Sharpeville Massacre in 1960 was part of the government's attempts to suppress the PAC, which was banned and driven into exile. In 1990, its legal status was restored. In general, the PAC has pursued its goals more violently and aggressively than the ANC has.

pass laws

A series of rules that restricted black South Africans from traveling outside of designated areas. The laws required each black man (and later each black woman) to carry a pass, or identification card. These passes enabled police to keep track of black people. The pass laws were repealed in 1986.

Rivonia Trial

A 1963-64 trial that resulted in Mandela's being sentenced to life imprisonment. Umkhonto we Sizwe, the guerrilla arm of the ANC, used a farm at Rivonia as a base. A police raid there captured documents proving that Mandela, who was already serving time on a different charge, had plotted to overthrow the government.

rondavel

A round native hut topped with thatch, or dried grass.

sanctions

The decision by one country to refuse to trade with another country. Sanctions were first called for by ANC president Albert Luthuli in the 1960s and were imposed in the 1970s and 1980s by the United States, Great Britain, the British Commonwealth, and the Common Market (now called the European Community). Following F. W. de Klerk's reforms, the international boycott on trade with South Africa began to be relaxed in 1990.

segregation
The separation of people, usually by race, although segregation by religion, sex, and economic standing also exists. Under a system of segregation, people of different groups cannot marry, attend the same schools, work at the same jobs, use the same transportation, belong to the same churches, shop in the same stores, or eat in the same restaurants. Apartheid is an extreme form of segregation.

Sobukwe, Robert (1924-78)
A teacher, black activist, organizer of the PAC, opponent of apartheid, and advocate of "Africa for Africans"; his goal was a United States of Africa made up of free black nations. Sobukwe persuaded his followers to peacefully break unjust laws, especially the pass laws.

Soweto
An acronym for SOuth WEst TOwnship, a black suburb located southwest of Johannesburg. Almost one million people, including the Mandelas, live in Soweto, with living conditions ranging from mansions to shacks.

Transkei
The "homeland" of the Xhosa people, located in southeastern South Africa. Transkei, which is home to about 2.5 million people, is Nelson Mandela's birthplace.

Umkhonto we Sizwe (Spear of the Nation)
The underground guerrilla branch of the ANC, organized by Nelson Mandela in 1960. Dedicated to the goal of overthrowing the rule of white South Africa, it began committing acts of sabotage designed to harm property but not people. After Mandela's imprisonment, it became a terrorist organization.

Verwoerd, Hendrik (1901-66)
The Afrikaner politician, who, as minister of native affairs and then prime minister, played a major role in instituting apartheid as South African government policy.

Chronology

1652   The first permanent white settlement is founded at Cape Town.

1795   Great Britain takes over Cape Colony during the Napoleonic Wars.

1835   Over ten thousand Boers leave Cape Colony and migrate in the "Great Trek" northeast, where they set up their own independent republics.

1893   Mahatma Gandhi arrives in South Africa to practice law. He becomes involved in protests against the pass laws and organizes the first passive resistance movement.

1899- In the Boer War, the Boer republics lose their independence and become
1902   British colonies.

1910	**May 31** — The Union of South Africa is formed from the merger of the British territories of Cape Colony and Natal with the conquered Boer republics. To pacify the Boers, the British deny blacks the vote or any other role in the new government.
1911	The Mines and Works Act introduces the idea of "job reservation" by forbidding blacks to hold management positions.
1912	**June 8** — The African National Congress is founded to unite all black South Africans, whatever their tribal origin, to protest their second-class citizenship.
1913	The Native Land Act is passed, setting aside less than 7 percent of South Africa's land for blacks, who at this point compose 67.3 percent of its people.
1918	**July 18** — Nelson Rolihlahla Mandela is born.
1923	New laws set up townships, all-black suburbs located near white towns.
1928	Henry Mandela, Nelson's father, dies. A distant relative, Jongintaba Dalindyebo, becomes ten-year-old Nelson's guardian.
1936	The Representation of Natives Act allows blacks to elect four (white) representatives to the South African parliament. The Natives' Representative Council is formed to advise the government, but its (black) members are given no power.
1938	Mandela enrolls at Fort Hare College, where he meets Oliver Tambo.
1939	**September** — World War II starts. South Africa enters on the Allied side.
1941	Mandela and his cousin Justice run away to Johannesburg. There, Mandela meets Walter Sisulu, who persuades him to join the ANC.
1942	Mandela gains his bachelor of arts degree. He enrolls at the University of the Witwatersrand to study law.
1943	The ANC Youth League is founded.
1944	Nelson Mandela marries Evelyn Mase.
1945	Thembi, the first of Evelyn and Nelson's four children, is born.
1947	Mandela is elected general secretary of the ANC Youth League.
1948	Makaziwe, the Mandelas' second child, is born, but dies nine months later. **May** — Prime Minister Jan Smuts is defeated in a close election by Dr. Daniel F. Malan's racist, pro-Afrikaner National party. Malan becomes the new prime minister and announces his new policy of apartheid. A series of repressive, antiblack laws quickly follows.
1949	Interracial marriages are made illegal.
1950	The Population Registration Act and the Group Areas Act are passed — the two basic laws for separating the country's people by race.

The Suppression of Communism Act bans the Communist party. This law is retroactive, imposing a jail sentence on anyone who has ever been a member. Makgatho, Evelyn and Nelson's second son, is born.
May 1 — The Communist party calls a strike to protest its banning. The police open fire, killing eighteen people.

1951   Mandela becomes president of the ANC Youth League.
A new law depriving Coloureds of the vote is ruled unconstitutional by South Africa's highest court.

1952   Chief Albert Luthuli becomes ANC president.
Mandela becomes president of the Transvaal branch of the ANC. He is appointed volunteer in chief of the Defiance Campaign, a nonviolent protest against unjust laws.

1953   Mandela and Oliver Tambo go into partnership as lawyers.
September – Mandela is banned. His banning orders require him to resign from the ANC and forbid him to attend any political meetings.

1954   Prime Minister Malan retires and is replaced by Johannes Strijdom, an even more extreme racist.
The Mandelas' fourth child is born and is named Makaziwe, after the daughter who died in infancy.

1955   **June** — The Congress of the People is held in Johannesburg. The delegates attending approve the Freedom Charter.

1956   **December 5** — Mandela is one of 156 people arrested and charged with high treason. The resulting four-year trial is known as the Treason Trial.

1957   Nelson and Evelyn Mandela are divorced.

1958   **June 14** — Mandela marries Winnie Nomzano Madikizela.
September — Strijdom dies, and Minister of Native Affairs Hendrik Verwoerd becomes prime minister.

1959   **February 4** — Winnie and Nelson's eldest child, Zeni, is born.
April — The Pan-Africanist Congress is formed.

1960   **March 21** — Robert Sobukwe and the PAC organize a massive, nationwide protest against the pass laws. Police open fire on unarmed demonstrators at Sharpeville, killing sixty-nine people and injuring 180.
March 30 — Mandela is arrested and imprisoned for five months.
April 8 — The ANC and PAC are banned.
December — Chief Albert Luthuli, banned president of the ANC, becomes the first African to be awarded the Nobel Peace Prize.
December 23 — Zindzi, Nelson and Winnie's second daughter, is born.

1961   **March 29** — The judge dismisses all charges against the last thirty-one defendants in the Treason Trial, including Mandela.
Mandela goes underground to continue ANC activities. He forms Umkhonto we Sizwe, a guerrilla movement.

May 31 — The Union of South Africa becomes the Republic of South Africa and withdraws from the British Commonwealth of Nations.

1962   **January** — Mandela tours Africa to get funds and support for the ANC from other newly independent African countries.
July 20 — Mandela returns to South Africa and is soon arrested. Later in the year, he is sentenced to five years' hard labor for leaving the country without a passport and for organizing strikes.

1963   **May** — Mandela is moved from the Pretoria Central prison to Robben Island.
July 11 — The police raid the secret Umkhonto we Sizwe headquarters on a farm near Rivonia, arresting Walter Sisulu and fifteen others. They find proof that Mandela founded the group and planned many of its activities.
October — Mandela is brought back to Pretoria to face charges of plotting the violent overthrow of the government.

1964   **June 11** — Mandela and other defendants are found guilty of sabotage and trying to cause a violent revolution. They are sentenced to life imprisonment.

1966   **September** — Prime Minister Verwoerd is stabbed to death on the floor of the South African parliament. John Vorster becomes the new prime minister.

1969   **May** — Winnie Mandela is arrested and charged with trying to revive the ANC. The following year, all charges are dropped, but Winnie and her twenty-one codefendants are immediately rearrested by police.

1973   Mandela is offered release from prison on the condition that he accept exile in the Transkei. He refuses.

1976   **June** — The Children's Revolt. Steven Biko's Black Consciousness movement inspires thousands of schoolchildren to protest having to use Afrikaans instead of their native languages in some classes in school.

1977   **May 16** — Winnie Mandela is banished to Brandfort.
August 18 — Steven Biko is arrested and later dies in his prison cell.

1978   Vorster resigns the office of prime minister. Pieter Willem (P. W.) Botha becomes the new prime minister and vows to dismantle apartheid.

1980   South African hotels, libraries, and restaurants are desegregated.

1983   A new constitution is adopted. It divides the South African parliament into three houses: the House of Assembly (for whites), the House of Delegates (for Asians), and the House of Representatives (for Coloureds). The country's black majority, however, is still excluded from representation and voting.

1985   The Mixed Marriages Act is repealed.
Forced removals of blacks from "white" areas are halted.
Botha offers to free Mandela on the condition that he renounce violence. Mandela refuses.

1986   The pass laws are repealed. South African citizenship is restored to all those deprived of it under the "homelands" program.

Winnie Mandela forms the Mandela Football Club as her private bodyguard. Over the next several years, she and members of the club are linked with a range of violent activities, including the murder of a boy, Stompie Moeketsi.

1989 **August** — Frederik Willem (F. W.) de Klerk replaces P. W. Botha as state president. De Klerk vows to end discriminatory laws and to seek a bill of rights for people of all races.
October 15 — De Klerk releases eight leading political prisoners, including Walter Sisulu.

1990 **February 2** — De Klerk announces the unbanning of the ANC, the PAC, the Communist party of South Africa, and other groups.
February 11 — Nelson Mandela is released from prison.
May 2 — Talks begin between de Klerk's government and the ANC to negotiate the transfer to black majority rule.
June-July — Mandela embarks on a fourteen-nation world tour.
July Several European nations announce that they will consider lifting economic sanctions against South Africa in response to de Klerk's reforms.
August — Jerry Richardson, head of the Mandela Football Club, is found guilty of the murder of Stompie Moeketsi and sentenced to death.
The ANC announces that it will stop its guerrilla warfare against the government. In return, de Klerk promises to end martial law and speeds up the release of political prisoners and the return of exiles.
September — Winnie Mandela is formally charged with kidnapping and torturing Stompie Moeketsi.
Violence breaks out between ANC supporters and Inkatha, the Zulu nationalist group, and over seven hundred people die.
November 29 — Mandela and South African archbishop Desmond Tutu meet, along with leaders of the PAC and several of the "homelands," to try to unite the different black groups.
December — Oliver Tambo, ANC president in exile, returns to South Africa for the first time in thirty years.

Index